MW00986612
To
From
Date

Your Childhood

Why did your parents choose the name you have?

Tell me a story that your parents shared about your toddler years.

Did you have a nickname?

Who gave it to you, and why?

What is one of the most important lessons you learned from your mother?

Share the best piece of advice that your father gave you.

What is your most cherished memory of your parents?

Describe your favorite family activity when you were younger.

When you were a child, what was your favorite game to play alone?

Who were some of your neighborhood friends?

Tell me about a particularly mischievous summer day with them.

Tell me a talent you discovered you had as a little girl.

What was something about you that everyone seemed to notice?

Were you more of a daydreamer or an outdoorsy child?

Describe a sad day for you during your girlhood.

What was elementary school like for you?

What television shows did you just have to watch?

What were the most popular songs of the day?

What films made your young imagination race?

What were your favorite books?

Why did you love them so?

Describe a special moment from your childhood.

How would you describe the different personalities of your brothers and sisters when they were younger?

Can you remember what sort of things caused you and your siblings to quarrel?

What is one nasty fight that you had, and how was it resolved?

Besides your parents and siblings, what family member were you closest to?

What is a cherished memory from that relationship?

Those Fleeting Teen Years and Early Adulthood

How did you feel on your first day of high school?

Describe the funniest date you ever went on.

What was the silliest thing you ever did in class?

Describe a typical day for you in high school.

What big news events filled the headlines when you were a teenager?

Did any news events worry you or make you sad?

Were there ever any issues of the day that you got involved in, be they political, social, or educational?

Describe the latest technological advances of the day.

What are some inventions I take for granted that you could never have dreamed of back then?

During your teen years, what did you think the future was going to be like?

Who were the celebrity heartthrobs during your teen years?

Did you have a favorite band?

How did their music make you feel?

What were your hopes and wishes for prom?

Who was your fantasy prom date?

What kind of house did you dream of living in one day?

Where did you want to live?

How is the current you similar to or different than the teenage you, in terms of personality and tendencies?

What was your first job?

What was the worst job you ever had?

Tell me about the best job you ever got.

Describe the first apartment or home that you lived in away from your family or college dorm.

How did it feel to be independent for the first time in your twenties?

Was being a responsible adult harder than you thought it would be?

Tell me about a troubling time you had in your early adulthood.

What was the hardest thing to get used to about being an adult?

What lessons did you learn as a teenager that served you well in early adulthood?

Tell me about a moment that made finally being an adult better than you ever dreamed possible.

You and Dad

Where did you meet my father?

Was it love at first sight?

What was the first thing you thought when you met my father?

What did he look like when you first saw him?

When was the moment you realized you wanted to marry Dad?

Tell me about your wedding day.

How did you feel when you were first married?

What is the nicest thing about being married to my dad?

Tell me about the best anniversary celebration that you and Dad ever had.

What is your favorite thing about Dad?

If you could change one little thing about him, what would it be?

What similar interests brought you and him together?

What interests do you and Dad share now?

What have been some important milestones in your marriage?

Describe a romantic time that you had together before you had children.

Which aspects of being married have surprised you?

Share a funny story from your first few years of marriage.

What was a stressful event in the early years?

Share a funny marriage story that happened recently.

What are the biggest obstacles that you and Dad have had to overcome with one another?

What is one thing you know that you and Dad will always agree on?

What is something that you often butt heads over?

What's the best way you've learned to ease a marital conflict?

How has being married enriched you?

Describe what sacrifices you've made for marriage.

What sacrifices have you made for love in general?

What marital advice would you pass on to me?

The Magic of Children and Family

How did you feel when you found out that you were going to be a mom?

Were you ever scared during your pregnancy?

What was the most fulfilling part of being pregnant?

How did Dad react when he discovered a child was on the way?

What special activities did you engage in to help the pregnancy along, like classes, exercises, or routines?

Were there any funny moments during visits to the doctor?

What goals did you lay out for yourself for being a good mother?

What sort of foods did you eat while you were pregnant with me?

Can you recognize any of the foods I love today as coming from that time?

What is one lesson you've learned about children and their mothers?

What is something you've learned about children and their fathers?

In what ways did you interact with me that you know were inspired by your relationship with your mother?

In what ways did you act differently than your mother in raising me?

Describe your feelings the first time you held me.

How did you choose my name?

When you saw me take my first step, how did you feel?

Are there ways that I remind you of yourself when you were the same age?

In what ways are we different?

Do you see any similarities between our family and yours when you were growing up?

What is one thing you'd like your children to remember about you?

What was your favorite part of watching me mature into who I am today?

What is some advice for raising a strong family?

What beliefs and priorities do you hope I instill in my children?

Given my personality, do you think I have similar child-raising instincts to yours?

What does our relationship mean to you and your life?

Notes